Getting Your Child Ready for Kindergarten

> *All I ever needed to know I learned in kindergarten.*
>
> —Robert Fulghum

Every year, more than three million children enter a kindergarten classroom for the first time. They are excited (and perhaps a little nervous). Their parents are proud (and perhaps feeling a little sentimental).

Each child comes equipped with strengths, weaknesses, skills, and needs. And on a momentous day like the first day of kindergarten, parents may be asking, "Is my child ready for school?" Sadly, for many children, the answer may be "no."

For years, research has shown that a huge learning gap already exists on the first day of kindergarten. Statistics collected by the Federal Interagency Forum on Child and Family Statistics show that many children—especially those from low-income families—are starting school with limited language skills, health problems, and social or emotional problems that interfere with their learning (2012). In their 2000 study on early childhood development, Jack P. Shonkoff and Deborah A. Phillips note, "Striking disparities in what children know and can do are evident well before they enter kindergarten. These differences are strongly associated with social and economic circumstances and they are predictive of subsequent academic performance" (p. 5).

Today, school readiness should not just be an issue for kindergarteners, their parents, and their teachers. It should be a concern of everyone in our nation.

This publication examines what we know about school readiness; discusses some of the reasons children are not ready; and outlines what schools, parents, and communities can do to help children enter school ready to learn.

The New Kindergarten Classroom

In the past, kindergarten was, quite literally, a "child's garden." Children came to school for a half-day program. The purpose of kindergarten was to get children ready for first grade, where the real academic work started.

The role of kindergarten has since changed. As early as the early 1990s, researchers found that kindergartens were focusing on a more narrow range of academic skills (Love et al., 1992). That trend has continued. Today, in many states, children are expected to be reading at least some common words by the end of the year. They also are asked to add numbers with sums less than ten. As the *San Diego Union-Tribune* put it, "Kindergarten is no longer about doing kid stuff" (Gao, 2005).

Unfortunately, that means that children who start school behind their peers have a hard time catching up. In fact, studies show that at least half of the educational achievement gaps that show up in the higher grades are already present when children walk in the door on their first day of kindergarten (Lee and Burkham, 2002). The larger the gap at school entry, the harder it is to close.

That's why "school readiness" involves much more than just the students. Families play a critical role in helping children get ready for school. Parents are still their children's first—and most important—teachers. When they surround their children with their love, their support, and opportunities to explore and learn, they give their children the gift of school readiness.

Schools, too, have a role to play. Students come to school speaking a variety of languages and with a wide range of experiences. Schools must be prepared to meet the needs of today's children and their families.

Finally, communities also play a critical role. They must support families, providing children with opportunities to learn, support for their families, and the services children need to be healthy and strong.

So it's important for everyone—parents, schools, and the community at large—to think about what it takes to help children be better prepared for the first day of school. If we want all children to be successful in school—and to grow into healthy and productive adults—then everyone has a stake in ensuring that our children are ready for school . . . and our schools are ready for our children.

What Do We Know about Readiness?

To Antonio, his first day of school seemed like a big adventure. When he walked into the classroom, he was happy to see some of the same children he played with in preschool and others from his neighborhood. The classroom was decorated with brightly colored letters and numbers. He knew some of them already—his mom had showed him that *A* was the first letter of his name.

There were things to climb on and move around, pictures of animals, and musical instruments to play. On the bookshelves, he saw some of the books his parents had read to him.

The time flew by as Antonio shared toys and games with other children and got to know his teacher. At the end of school, he was bubbling with news for his parents, who listened as he told them about his exciting first day.

Zoe was frightened when she entered the classroom for the first time. She had never seen so many other children in the same room. She wasn't sure how long she would have to stay or why she was even there. The teacher was a stranger, and though she tried, Zoe couldn't seem to follow her directions very well. When the teacher read a story, she had trouble sitting still. She didn't know that people read books for fun.

By 9:30, Zoe was hungry and couldn't concentrate. She hadn't eaten any breakfast because her mother had to leave early to go to work.

She tried to be brave, but a little boy teased her because she couldn't catch a ball. She cried for a long time.

Although Antonio and Zoe are fictional, they represent a few of the feelings and experiences of children entering school for the first time. Either could have come from a poor or a wealthy background or a single-parent, divorced, blended, or nuclear family.

The difference is that in these stories, Antonio had some preparation before he started school. He was more *ready* to be a student than Zoe. While this is no guarantee of academic success, studies have shown a strong tie between the level of a child's readiness to enter school and student achievement.

Basically, the emphasis on "school readiness" is nothing more than common sense. A child who is comfortable with other children, has some familiarity with learning and listening, is patient, and is well-fed and healthy is a step ahead of a child who comes to school lacking any or all of these advantages. To young children, being even a little behind can lead to feelings of inadequacy and failure that haunt them throughout their schooling. On the other hand, it makes sense that children who enter school confidently are better able to develop and keep a lifelong love of learning.

In the past, children were thought to be ready for school if they had certain *skills*—for example, if they could recite the alphabet, count to ten, recognize colors, and tie their shoes. Today, educators and parents know children need more than a list of accomplishments to succeed in school and in life.

Children's readiness for school depends on a number of factors. They must be *healthy*—because children who are tired, hungry, or sick cannot concentrate. They need the ability to *speak and listen,* because reading is the foundation of all other learning. They need *self-esteem* so they can keep working when a task is difficult. They need *self-control,* because things will not always go their way. And they need to *cooperate with others,* because students cannot have the undivided attention of their teacher (Emrig, Moore, and Scarupa, 2001).

How do children develop the characteristics that lead to school success? There is no single answer. But we know some things are more likely to help prepare children for the first day of kindergarten.

The Impact of Preschool

There is no question that today's families face many problems. Joblessness, drugs and alcohol, physical and sexual abuse, and persistent poverty are just some of the troubles that take their toll on parents' ability to provide the support their children need.

Yet despite these difficult realities, concerned communities have made vital differences in the lives of children. There is evidence that disadvantages can be overcome, and all children can start school ready to learn. Preschool plays a significant role in preparing children.

Researchers at the University of Minnesota followed more than 1,400 families whose children were enrolled in Chicago's Child-Parent Center, a high-quality preschool program. All families were economically disadvantaged; most lived in neighborhoods of persistent poverty.

Researchers followed these students and a similar group of children who did not attend preschool. The results were striking—even twenty-five years later. The preschool participants:

✓ were more likely to graduate from high school on time

✓ had higher rates of college attendance

✓ worked in higher-paying jobs

✓ were less likely ever to have been arrested

✓ had lower rates of substance abuse.

Preschool participants whose parents were high school dropouts showed even larger advantages compared with non-preschool peers (Reynolds et al., 2011).

This is one of the largest and longest-running studies of the impact of preschool. The lesson is clear: Preschool can have a lifelong impact.

An Investment in the Future

James Heckman, a University of Chicago economist, and Dimitriy Masterov, from the University of Michigan (2007), have taken an economic look at the impact of a high-quality preschool program. They used data from the Perry Preschool Project, one of the earliest and most comprehensive studies of the impact of preschool. The authors estimate the rate of return for programs like the Perry Project to be a substantial 16 percent. Some of the payback goes directly to the preschool participants in the form of higher wages throughout their life. But about three-fourths of the benefit goes to society—in lower crime and savings on prison spending.

What Parents Can Do

As the child's most important teacher, a parent plays the biggest role in preparing a child for school. Of course, there is never a time when a child is *not* ready to learn. From the first day, babies are exploring the world around them. They listen and watch. They learn about cause (I cry) and effect (I get fed).

Toddlers begin to walk and explore space. They learn with all their senses. And while they are learning, they are also mastering new words and building the foundation that will eventually help them at school.

More Than the Three "Rs"

Readiness for school involves much more than academic knowledge and skills. Even children who are the same age may vary widely in how ready they are for kindergarten. The Fairfax County, Virginia, schools advise parents to focus on their own child, not on what other children are doing. "Children learn, grow, and develop at different rates. Differences can be observed in children of the same age who may vary in their ability to perform certain physical, social, or intellectual tasks" (Department of Instructional Services, n.d.).

However, there are some signals of school readiness. Children who are ready to learn should:

✓ be curious, active, and eager to learn

✓ take pride in their ability to do things for themselves, whether that means tying their shoes, putting things away, or controlling their behavior

✓ want to please others

✓ be able to express themselves in words

✓ ask questions about how things work and the world around them

✓ believe they can learn.

Parents play the most critical role in ensuring that their children start school ready to learn. For a mother, these responsibilities begin before her child is born. By eating nutritious food and receiving prenatal care, mothers are helping their babies begin life on the right track, free from illnesses and other health problems. Parents' contributions continue throughout the early years, when they provide a loving, healthy environment in which children can grow and develop.

Talk, Listen, Love

Language, without question, is the key to a child's learning. It is tied to everything a child learns or does in school. Children who fail to develop adequate speech and language skills in the first years of life are more likely to experience reading problems in school than those who receive adequate stimulation (Clapp, 1988).

Talk to your child—even when you think he is too young to understand what you are saying. Describe your surroundings. "Look at the blue flower! Listen to the bird's song." This is how children learn the words to describe the world around them.

Some children come to school knowing far fewer words than others. By the time children from economically advantaged families are three years old, they have a substantially more varied vocabulary than do children from low-income families. Research shows low-income children knew 600 fewer words than children the same age from families with upper incomes (Hart and Risley, 1995). By grade 2, the gap widens to about 4,000 words (Biemiller and Slonim, 2001).

It is also important that you pay attention to what your child is trying to tell you. When you listen to your child (even if you think it is just "baby talk"), you are sending a message that she is important, that she is worthwhile. Make sure your body language shows you are listening, too. Face your child when she is talking, and don't simply nod while you are doing other things. These are good ways to build your child's listening and speaking skills, as well as her self-esteem.

Have you hugged your child today?

Physical contact—especially hugging or touching—helps children thrive. In one landmark study, premature infants were given gentle massages several times a day. These babies gained 47 percent more weight, were more active and alert, and had shorter hospital stays than infants who were left alone (Field et al., 1986).

Immunize Your Child

Routine checkups at your doctor's office or local health clinic are the best way to keep children healthy—even if they aren't sick. By ensuring that your child gets immunized on schedule, you can provide the best defense against dangerous childhood diseases that can cause school absences and limit children's ability to achieve in school.

Immunizing doesn't just keep your own child healthy; it also keeps every child in your community healthy by controlling outbreaks of diseases.

Most children receive some immunizations, but not all are fully immunized. Check with your doctor or a health clinic to find out whether your child has all the immunizations needed. You can also find out the latest recommendations on the Centers for Disease Control website (www.cdc.gov/vaccines).

If you follow the recommended schedule for immunizations, you will be protecting your child against these diseases:

✓ bacterial meningitis

✓ diphtheria

✓ hepatitis A

✓ hepatitis B

✓ influenza

✓ measles

✓ mumps

✓ pertussis (whooping cough)

✓ pneumococcal disease

✓ polio

✓ rubella (German measles)

✓ tetanus (lockjaw)

✓ rotavirus

✓ varicella (chickenpox).

If you don't have a pediatrician, call your local public health department. It usually has supplies of vaccines and may give free immunizations. As always, *you should always consult with your health care provider.* There may be variations in treatment that your pediatrician recommends based on the individual facts and circumstances.

Socialize Your Child

Children must also be *socially* ready for school. They need to get along with other children and with adults. They must be able to adapt to a daily classroom routine and to share attention with other children.

Parents can help their children get ready for school by giving them a chance to be a part of a group of children. That might be in a preschool, but it could also be a play group, at day care, or in a church program.

Children who are used to spending some time away from their parents and in the company of other children are more likely to adjust well to being part of a class. There may be twenty-five or thirty other children in their kindergarten—so the teacher can't focus just on your child every minute.

Children also need to know how to:

✓ take turns

✓ share

✓ make compromises

✓ control their emotions and anger

✓ approach unfamiliar children

✓ follow class rules

✓ finish what they start

✓ do things for themselves (put on a coat or jacket, use the restroom, wash hands)

✓ follow the teacher's directions

✓ be generally nice to others.

Build Coordination

Children need physical skills to be successful in school. They need *fine motor skills* so they can hold a pencil, button their own clothing, or tie their shoes. They need *large muscle control* so they can run, jump, and climb. And they need *self-care skills* so they can take responsibility for themselves and their belongings in the classroom. All these are things parents teach naturally.

As your child learns to use his muscles in new ways, help him practice a skill over and over. For example, color or draw with your child, or toss a ball back and forth in the yard. You can even help develop a baby's coordination by playing patty cake or building a block tower. In this way, you teach him to concentrate and help lengthen his attention span. Both are important for success in school. As a rule of thumb, by age two, a child can be expected to concentrate on a task for as long as ten minutes. By age six, your child may be content when doing a single activity for a half-hour or more.

Other simple childhood activities can pay off in later learning benefits. When your child strings beads, she's helping her eyes and hands work together—a skill she'll use someday in writing. When he plays follow the leader, he's learning to be part of a group.

Physical activity and coordination are important for boys and girls. Sometimes without meaning to, parents teach boys and girls stereotyped physical activities. In fact, both benefit from a wide range of activities such as throwing and kicking a ball, dancing, jumping rope, swimming, and working puzzles.

The academic connection

When we read, our eyes move from left to right. Young children need to be taught to develop this left-to-right progression naturally. If you are putting away the silverware, have your child sort from left to right. When you are reading to your child, sometimes move your fingers under the words.

Promote Responsibility

Children need emotional skills to be successful in school. One of the most important is responsibility—for their own behavior, for their possessions, for the books and objects in their classroom.

How do you teach responsibility?: by avoiding doing things your child can do for herself. Allow your toddler to feed herself (and accept that mealtime will be messy and s-l-o-w). Let your toddler choose which shirt she wants to wear (and don't worry if she chooses the polka dot shirt to go with the checked pants). Encourage your preschooler to choose the crayons she wants to use in her coloring book (and get ready to see a purple horse and a red elephant).

These all seem like small choices. But they are ways your child can practice making decisions and then living with the consequences. They will help her learn how to take on bigger choices as she grows older.

Readiness for school does not mean that your child will do everything right. Rather, it means that she takes pleasure in learning how to do things for herself. If you always do everything for your child, and always tell her what to do, she will not be able to make her own decisions or learn how to be independent.

Raise a Reader

Retired elementary school principal George Towery spent thirty-nine years observing what helps children be successful in school. He found one factor that was more important than any other. "The best thing a parent can ever do with their child is read. There is no substitute," he says. "Read with your preschooler. Read as your child is learning to sound out words. Read long after kids can read for themselves" (personal communication, September 23, 2008).

His practical experience is confirmed by research. A National Center for Education Statistics report summarized the results of many studies: "For decades, research has shown that children whose parents read to them become better readers and do better in school" (Nord et al., 1999, p. 1).

The results are remarkable. Of the children who were read to three or more times in the past week by a family member:

✓ 42 percent could recognize all their letters, count at least to 20, and write their name, compared with just 24 percent of children who had been read to three or fewer times in the last week

✓ 26 percent recognized all their letters, compared to 14 percent who were read to less than three times in the past week (Nord et al., 1999).

Set aside some time each day to read aloud with your child. Bedtime stories are a tradition in many families. But if that time doesn't work for you, find another time to read. Some busy parents read while their children are eating breakfast. Others set aside time right after dinner. Whatever time works best for your family, make this a daily habit. It will soon be one of your favorite times of the day.

Here are some other ways you can help your child develop the skills that will help him become a reader:

✓ Look for simple signs you can read. "Look at this sign on the door—it says 'Exit.' It is the way out.") Look for the signs on a favorite store or restaurant. ("The sign says, 'Annie's Bakery.'")

✓ Occasionally, trace a word with your finger as you are reading aloud.

✓ Point to the top of a page during read-aloud, saying, "Here's where we start."

✓ Sometimes, let your child open the book you are reading. Let him find the first word on the first page.

Limit "Screen Time"

The American Academy of Pediatrics (AAP) recommends that parents limit combined "screen time"—time spent watching television, DVDs, computers, and video games—should be limited to no more than two hours per day for preschool-age children. In a study published in the *Journal of Pediatrics*, researchers found that most children—66 percent—exceeded that daily amount (Tandon et al., 2010).

Children who spend too much time staring at a screen are not reading. They are not playing. They are not talking with others. Problems that grow out of too much television viewing include speech delays, aggressive behavior, and obesity.

Here are ways you can limit your child's "screen time":

✓ Plan your screen time. Don't have the TV on from morning until night. Help your child choose the programs he will watch. Keep the set off at other times.

✓ Use the DVR or video recorder. That way, you can choose when your child watches a favorite program. You can also, if you wish, fast-forward through commercials for products or other programs you do not wish your child to see.

✓ Talk about what you saw. Ask your child to tell you a new word he learned from a TV show. Or have him make up his own story about a favorite character from a TV show.

✓ Go to the library to look for books that talk about the subject of some of your child's favorite shows. Or help her cut out pictures from magazines and write her own book that is based on a TV show.

✓ Make certain that TV isn't used as a babysitter. Instead, balance good television with other enjoyable activities for your child.

Develop Self-Control

In the late 1960s, researchers conducted a fascinating study on self-control in young children. The subjects were offered a cookie or a marshmallow as a treat. The researcher said that if they wanted to eat the treat right now, they could choose one. But if they could wait a few minutes while the researcher left the room, they could have two treats.

The temptation was hard to resist, but some children, even those who were very young, managed to wait so they could eat a second treat.

Years later, the researchers learned something surprising. The children who had the self-control to wait for a few minutes were more successful than the children who gobbled down the treat right away. They did better in school. They went to better colleges. They got better jobs (Lehrer, 2009). The self-control they displayed at a young age helped them throughout their life.

Self-control is also important for children in the classroom. One teacher can't always answer a child's question right away. Children can't go outside to play whenever they feel like it. And if they get upset, they have to know how to calm themselves down and behave in appropriate ways.

Parents can help children learn how to develop self-control. One way is by helping children see the connection between their actions and the consequences of those actions. If two children are fighting over a toy, the consequence is that the toy will be put away for a while. If a child loses his temper, he may have to sit quietly on the stairs for a few minutes until he can calm himself down.

Parents also teach children self-control by expecting children to wait sometimes for what they want. This is called *delayed gratification.* "We're not eating sweets now. Dinner is in a few minutes. We'll have dessert after we eat."

Make Learning—and School—Sound Fun

When you talk about school, let your child know that she will enjoy learning. Your positive attitude is sure to help shape your child's feelings.

In the weeks before school, there are some things you can do to ease the transition:

✓ Visit the school. Many schools have a special day for kindergarten children. It gives them a chance to learn the basics—where their classroom is located, where the bus lets them off, where they will eat lunch. Watch for this day at your school and be sure to attend with your child.

✓ Play "What If?" Ask questions about things that might happen in school.

  ✓ What if I don't get to sit with my best friend? (Teachers sometimes ask children to sit in certain seats. You can talk with your friend later.)

Sometimes, reading a book about kindergarten can make the first day of school seem a little more familiar. Barb Tigges, a counselor at Jordan Creek Elementary School in West Des Moines, Iowa, has prepared this comprehensive list of books you might read during the summer before kindergarten (used with permission):

Miss Bindergarten Gets Ready for Kindergarten (Joseph Slate)

The Kissing Hand (Audrey Penn)

Wemberly Worried (Kevin Henkes)

Froggy Goes to School (Jonathan London)

Countdown to Kindergarten (Alison McGhee)

First Day Jitters (Julie Danneberg)

The Night before Kindergarten (Natasha Wing)

When You Go to Kindergarten (James Howe)

Will I Have a Friend? (Miriam Cohen)

Look Out Kindergarten, Here I Come (Nancy Carlson)

Emily's First 100 Days of School (Rosemary Wells)

Welcome to Kindergarten (Anne Rockwell)

Kindergarten Rocks! (Katie Davis)

Tiptoe into Kindergarten (Jacqueline Rogers)

Tom Goes to Kindergarten (Margaret Wild)

Annabelle Swift, Kindergartener (Amy Schwartz)

If You Take a Mouse to School (Laura Numeroff)

My Kindergarten (Rosemary Wells)

I Am Too Absolutely Small for School! (Lauren Child)

The Twelve Days of Kindergarten: A Counting Book (Deborah Lee Rose)

Kindergarten Count to 100 (Jacqueline Rogers)

✓ What if I have a question about something I don't understand? (All kids have questions. It's how they learn. Raise your hand and wait for the teacher to call on you.)

✓ What if the teacher asks me a question and I don't know the answer? (You're not expected to know everything on the first day of school—you're going to school to learn. Just tell the teacher you don't know the answer to that question.)

✓ Get on a "school schedule" for about a week before the first day. In many families, that means going to bed a little earlier and getting up earlier.

✓ Be positive. Parents are sometimes sentimental about the start of school. Keep a positive attitude. Say things like, "You're going to be just fine. I will see you right after school is over."

✓ Together, choose a small, tangible object your child can wear or keep in a pocket as a reminder of your love. This can be a photo, a small piece of jewelry like a pin, ring, or necklace, or even a rock or a shell.

Gift of Time versus Learning-By-Doing

During the past decade, it has become more common for parents to hold their kids out of school for an extra year. Nationally, about 9 percent of parents hold their children out for an extra year. Some schools and districts also recommend a delayed entry into school. Typically, kids who are redshirted are more likely to be boys or to have birthdays in the last half of the year, according to the National Center for Education Statistics (West, Meek, and Hurst, 2000).

Parents who hold their kids out (or schools that make redshirting an easy option) do so because they think it gives these kids an advantage. They hope children will be more ready for school—academically, physically, and socially. And, for a while, redshirting appears to give children an academic boost. Older kindergarteners score on average 24 percentage points higher on standardized reading tests than their younger classmates.

But over time, those gains start to erode. By eighth grade, the younger students have virtually caught up—older students score just 4 points higher. A study in the *Journal of Human Resources* suggests the trade-offs aren't worth it (University of Illinois at Urbana-Champaign, 2008).

What does this mean for parents? Think carefully before you keep your child out of school for an extra year. Many experts, including the National Association for the Education of Young Children and the National Association of Elementary School Principals, believe that children are helped more when they are in an environment that stimulates and challenges them.

What Schools Can Do

There has always been a lot of talk about what it takes to get children ready for school. But shouldn't there also be a focus on how to get schools ready for children?

After all, the definition of what it means to be "ready for school" can vary from state to state, district to district, and even from school to school. Children are not required to attend kindergarten in every state. According to the Education Commission of the States, just forty-five states or territories require districts to provide either a half-day or a full-day kindergarten program, and just nineteen states or territories require children to attend (Bush, 2011).

So in a growing number of communities, "readiness" is now viewed as a responsibility that should be shared by parents, schools, and the community. Rather than adopting a one-size-fits-all approach to teaching and learning, the notion of "ready schools" begins with the belief that programs should be fine tuned to fit the needs of the children. If existing practices and programs don't benefit the children who are enrolled, they should be modified or even abandoned (Gonzales, 2002).

This means that schools need to build partnerships to support children and their families. Schools and community agencies can work together to be sure children have access to health care, nutrition, and social services. Ready schools can also establish partnerships with parents and other community organizations and institutions—community colleges, universities, museums, libraries—to provide families with out-of-school enrichment opportunities for children (Gonzales, 2002; Shore, 1998).

In *Ready Schools* (1998), the National Education Goals Panel outlined the characteristics schools need to be prepared for all children. According to the panel, ready schools do the following:

✓ Smooth the transition between home and school. Children are more successful if the welcome begins before the bell rings on the first day of school.

✓ Strive for continuity between early care and education programs and elementary schools.

✓ Help children learn and make sense of their complex and exciting world. They help children master literacy, numeracy, and other skills, and then use those skills to explore and learn about the world around them.

✓ Commit to the success of every child. They are sensitive to the needs of individual children, including the effects of poverty, race, and disability.

✓ Commit to the success of every teacher and every adult who interacts with children during the school day. They give teachers the time to develop their skills and their practice.

✓ Introduce or expand approaches that have been shown to raise achievement. These include parent involvement, flexible staffing, and early intervention for struggling students.

✓ Act as learning organizations that alter practices and programs if they do not benefit children.

✓ Serve children in communities. Schools alone cannot meet the needs of children and families.

✓ Take responsibility for results. They challenge every child. They regularly report on student progress.

✓ Have strong leadership. Successful schools depend on the vision and leadership of outstanding school leaders.

The Harvard Family Research Project notes the critical importance of involving parents of kindergarten students. Specifically, they say that schools must do the following:

✓ Reach out. Schools need to reach out to families of preschool children.

✓ Reach back. This communication needs to begin well before the children show up for school on the first day of kindergarten.

✓ Reach with appropriate intensity. Schools should use a range of techniques—from home visits to websites—to communicate with the widest possible range of families (Bohan-Baker and Little, 2002).

What Communities Must Do

Many states and local communities have developed innovative programs to ensure that all children will be ready to learn. These range from preschool programs for children to parent education programs.

Here are some examples of what communities are doing:

WORKPLACE PARENT EDUCATION

Sometimes, parents are so overwhelmed by their responsibilities of earning a living and raising their families that they can't find time to do anything else. This was the case in Howard County, Maryland, so the school went to the parents.

Because of turmoil in their home country of Myanmar, a large number of refugees were settled in this suburban community. The parents found work at a local food packing company. But their opportunities to learn about their new country—and the schools their children would attend—were limited.

Now, the school district and the employer work in a partnership to provide on-site English language classes. But the classes go well beyond learning English. During one class, an immigration official talked with parents about how they could discuss problems with a landlord. A police officer came to the class to assure parents that they need not fear U.S. law enforcement.

The contact with the school has proved invaluable for both parents and educators. Parents now know how and when to register their children for school. And if there's ever a problem, they also know how to contact the principal—who has also been a visitor to their class (Samuels, 2011).

Countdown to Kindergarten

Countdown to Kindergarten is a year-long program designed to help Boston families with preschoolers get ready for kindergarten. Starting in September the year before children enroll, parents receive registration information, calls from volunteers, and written information on how they can enhance their child's learning at home. They are also invited to visit schools, take part in neighborhood kindergarten days, and attend a kindergarten celebration at the Boston Museum. Through the Talk, Read, Play program, parents can receive a Milestones guide in one of eight languages. They also visit a website that includes an up-to-date calendar of prekindergarten events and an opportunity to sign up to receive child development information through email or text messages. In the summer before children start kindergarten, they receive a free "I'm Going to Kindergarten" T-shirt at their local public library. It entitles them to free admission to select activities throughout the summer.

Mobile Classroom

The Plano, Texas, schools have always offered parent classes in the evenings. But a lack of transportation limited the numbers of parents who could take part.

So the district decided to bring the classroom to where the parents were. Using grant money, the school district purchased and equipped a customized motor home equipped with a dozen computers.

The mobile classroom schedules regular visits to low-income apartment complexes, Plano community centers, local churches, and mobile home sites. Painted on the side of the bus is this statement: "When we look at a student . . . we see a family."

The mobile classroom offers parent courses in computer literacy, finance, career exploration, and English. Parents are also able to access the school district's Parent Portal and learn about community resources. Before the arrival of the mobile classroom, parents had to travel to a central location to take advantage of these services, and many could not come.

Principals and teachers encouraged the district to establish the mobile classroom. By reaching parents, especially the low-income students served by Title I, the district is also impacting the children's abilities to learn and prosper.

HOME-BASED LEARNING FOR CHILDREN WITH DISABILITIES

Children with disabilities face special challenges as they prepare for school. In Portage, Wisconsin, a home-based program has helped families of young children with disabilities for more than forty years.

A home visitor works with parents to develop Individual Education Plan (IEP) and Individual Family Service Plan (IFSP) goals for each child. The home visitor takes into account the child's needs, the family's goals for the child, and the family's ability to provide support for the child.

Together, the home visitor and the parents develop basic routines and activities the parents can engage in every day. Specific play-based activities are also developed to help children reach their learning goals. The program has a long record of preparing children for school and for overall success (Barakat, Drylie, and Nash, 2004).

A BETTER CHANCE (ABC)

Given the extensive research on the importance of high-quality pre-school programs, many states have developed their own early childhood programs. In Arkansas, the A Better Chance (ABC) program has been in operation since 1991.

ABC serves children from birth through age five from low-income families. Other children who have risk factors, including being in foster care, having developmental delays or low birth weight, or having a teen parent, can also qualify for the program. Classes are offered in public schools, education cooperatives, and more traditional pre-school programs such as Head Start.

Because the program has been in existence for many years, research-ers have strong evidence of ABC's impact. Children enrolled in the program have

✓ An increase in their vocabulary scores of 31 percent more growth over the year due to the program. This improvement translates into an additional four months of progress in vocabulary growth due to the preschool program.

✓ Higher math scores on basic math skills like basic number con-cepts, simple addition and subtraction, telling time, and counting money. ABC children demonstrated 37 percent more growth over the year due to the program.

✓ Greater print awareness. Children enrolled in the program know more letters, more letter-sound associations and are more familiar with words and book concepts. They more than doubled expected growth due to the program (Hustedt et al., 2007).

PARENT-CHILD ACTIVITIES

In St. Cloud, Minnesota, the Early Childhood Family Education program involves both parents and children in a high-quality learn-ing experience.

During each two-hour session, parents and children will play together. Activities include art, music, story books, and other age-appropriate toys and activities. Then children work with an early childhood educator on a variety of learning activities while parents observe how the teacher is working with their child. Finally, parents have a chance to discuss what they have learned in an informal con-versation led by an early childhood educator.

The district offers a wide range of parent-child activities. There are even classes held after work for parents. Children are served a snack, and the classes end with a "wind-down" circle that the district prom-ises will send children home relaxed and ready for bed.

The programs are available to all parents in the district. Fees are based on family income, and no one is turned away because of an inability to pay.

The National Association for the Education of Young Children notes that the best community programs share three characteristics:

✓ They provide comprehensive services to meet a wide range of individual needs

✓ They strengthen the parents' role in supporting their child's development and learning

✓ They provide a wide array of firsthand experiences and learning activities to children, either directly or by teaching their parents new skills (NAEYC, 1995).

Conclusion

Our nation needs every child to be successful, right from the start. By working together, parents, schools, and communities can ensure that this essential goal becomes a reality . . . for all our nation's children.

Ready for School? A Checklist

Deciding whether a child is ready for school is a decision that will vary, child by child and family by family. But here's a checklist that can help you think it through.

How Is Your Child's General Health?

My child:

____ Eats a balanced diet

____ Gets plenty of rest

____ Receives regular medical and dental care

____ Has had all the necessary immunizations

____ Runs, jumps, plays outdoors, and does other activities that help develop his large muscles and provide exercise

____ Works puzzles, scribbles, colors, paints, and does other activities that help develop her small muscles

SOCIAL AND EMOTIONAL PREPARATION

My child:

___ Is learning to explore and try new things

___ Is learning to work well alone and to do many tasks for himself

___ Has many opportunities to be with other children and is learning to cooperate with them

___ Is curious and is motivated to learn

___ Is learning to finish tasks

___ Is learning to use self-control

___ Can follow simple instructions

___ Helps with family chores

LANGUAGE AND GENERAL KNOWLEDGE

My child:

___ Has many opportunities to talk and listen

___ Is read to every day

___ Has access to books and other reading materials

___ Is learning about print and books

___ Has his television viewing monitored by an adult

___ Is encouraged to ask questions

___ Is encouraged to solve problems

___ Has opportunities to notice similarities and differences

___ Is encouraged to sort and classify things

___ Is learning to write her name and address

___ Is learning to count and plays counting games

___ Is learning to identify and name shapes and colors

___ Has opportunities to draw, listen to, and make music and to dance

___ Has opportunities to get first-hand experiences to do things in the world—to see and touch objects, hear new sounds, smell and taste foods and watch things move

References

Barakat, R., Drylie, L., and Nash, J. (2004). The Portage Project: An overview of a model for early childhood education. Retrieved on July 3, 2011, from faculty.unlv.edu/jgelfer/ECE707/ThePortageProject(GROUP).doc.

Biemiller, A., and Slonim, N. (2001). Estimating root word vocabulary growth in normative and advantaged populations: Evidence for a common sequence of vocabulary acquisition. *Journal of Educational Psychology, 93,* 498–520

Bohan-Baker, R., and Little, M.D.R. (2002). The transition to kindergarten: A review of current research and promising practices to involve families. Boston: Harvard Family Research Project. Retrieved from www.hfrp.org/publications-resources/browse-our -publications/the-transition-to-kindergarten-a-review-of-current -research-and-promising-practices-to-involve-families.

Bush, M. (2011). State characteristics: Kindergarten. Denver, CO: Education Commission of the States. Retrieved from www.ecs.org/clearinghouse/90/71/9071.pdf.

Clapp, G. (1988). *Child study research: Current perspectives and applications.* Lexington, MA: Lexington Books.

Department of Instructional Services. (n.d.). Fairfax County's philosophy of early childhood education. Fairfax, VA: Fairfax County Public Schools. Retrieved from www.fcps.edu/is/earlychildhood/kindergarten/learnmore.shtml.

Emrig, C., Moore, A., and Scarupa, H. J. (Eds.). (2001). School readiness: Helping communities get children ready for school and schools ready for children. Washington, DC: Child Trends. Retrieved from www.childtrends.org/files/schoolreadiness.pdf.

Federal Interagency Forum on Child and Family Statistics. (2012). America's children: Key national indicators of well-being 2012. Washington, DC: Federal Interagency Forum on Child and Family Statistics. Retrieved from childstats.gov/americaschildren/famsoc .asp.

Field, T., Schanberg, S. M., Scafidi, F., Bauer, C. R., Vega-Lehr, N., Garcia, R., Nystrom, J., and Kuhn, C. M. (1986). Tactile/

kinesthetic stimulation effects on preterm neonates. *Pediatrics, 77*, 654–58.

Gao, H. (2005, April 11). Critics say pressure is too much; backers say preparation needed. *San Diego Union-Tribune*. Retrieved from legacy.utsandiego.com/news/education/20050411-9999-1n11kinder.html.

Gonzalez, R. (2002). *Ready schools: Practices to support the development and educational success of young children*. Los Angeles: UCLA Center for Healthier Children, Families, and Communities.

Hart, B., and Risley, T. (1995). *Meaningful differences in the everyday experience of young children*. Baltimore: Brookes.

Heckman, J. J. and Masterov, D.V. (2007). The productivity argument for investing in young children. Retrieved from jenni.uchicago.edu/human-inequality/papers/Heckman_final_all_wp_2007-03-22c_jsb.pdf.

Helping Your Preschool Child. (2005). Washington, DC: U.S. Department of Education. Retrieved from www2.ed.gov/parents/academic/help/preschool/brochure.html.

Hustedt, J. T., Barnett, W. S., Jung, K., and Thomas, J. (2007). The effects of the Arkansas Better Chance program on young children's school readiness. New Brunswick, NJ: National Institute for Early Education Research, Rutgers University. Retrieved from nieer.org/resources/research/PreschoolLastingEffects.pdf.

Lee, V., and Burkham, D. (2002). *Inequality at the starting gate: Social background differences in achievement as children begin school*. Washington, DC: Economic Policy Institute. Retrieved from www.epi.org/publication/books_starting_gate/.

Lehrer, J. (2009, May 18). Don't: The secret of self-control. *New Yorker*. Retrieved from www.newyorker.com/reporting/2009/05/18/090518fa_fact_lehrer.

Love, J. M., Logue, M. E., Trudeau, J. V., and Thayer, K. (1992). *Transitions to kindergarten in American schools: Final report of the National Transition Study*. Washington, DC: U.S. Department of Education.

Maxwell, K., and R. M. Clifford (2004). Research in review: School readiness assessment. *Young Children, 59*(1), 42–46.

National Association for the Education of Young Children (1995). *School readiness: A position statement of the National Association for the Education of Young Children*. Retrieved from www.naeyc.org/positionstatements/school_readiness.

National Education Goals Panel (1998). *Ready Schools.* Washington, DC: National Education Goals Panel.

Nord, C. W., Lennon, J., Liu, B., and Chandler, K. (1999). *Home literacy activities and signs of children's emerging literacy, 1999.* Washington, DC: National Center for Education Statistics. Retrieved from nces.ed.gov/pubs2000/2000026.pdf.

Reynolds, A. J., Temple, J. A., Ou, S., Arteaga, I., and White, B. A. B. (2011, June 9). School-based early childhood education and age-28 well-being: Effects by timing, dosage, and subgroups. *Sciencexpress.* Retrieved from www.sciencemag.org/content/early/2011/06/08/science.1203618.

Samuels, R. (2011, July 4). For Burmese refugees, English lessons at work build school ties. *Washington Post.* Retrieved from articles.washingtonpost.com/2011-06-30/local/35265607_1_burmese-refugees-english-lessons-refugees-work.

Shonkoff, J., and Phillips, D. (Eds.). (2000). *From neurons to neighborhoods: The science of early childhood development.* Washington, DC: National Academy of Sciences Press.

Shore, R. (1998). Ready schools: A report of the Goal 1 Ready Schools Resource Group. Washington, DC: The National Education Goals Panel.

Stillman, L., and Blank, R. K. (2008). Key state education policies on PK–12 education: 2008. Washington, D.C.: Council of Chief State School Officers. Retrieved from www.ccsso.org/Documents/2008/Key_State_Education_Policies_2008.pdf.

Tandon, P. S., Zhou, C., Lozano, P., and Christakis, D. (2011) Preschoolers' total daily screen time at home and by type of child care. *Journal of Pediatrics, 58*(2), 297–300.

University of Illinois at Urbana-Champaign. (2008, August 18). Starting kindergarten later gives students only a fleeting edge. *ScienceDaily.* Retrieved from www.sciencedaily.com/releases/2008/08/080818184420.htm.

Vogt, J. Starting kindergarten: Helping your child off to a positive experience. Urbandale, IA: Waukee Public Schools. Retrieved from www.waukee.k12.ia.us/walnuthillselementary/guidance/Smoothtransitiontokdg.pdf.

West, J., Meek, A., and Hurst, D. (2000). Children who enter kindergarten late or repeat kindergarten: Their characteristics and later school performance. (NCES No. 2000-039). Washington, DC: U.S. Department of Education.